Intentions For the Spiritually Aware Parent

Christina Fletcher

The author of this book does not dispense medical advice or
prescribe the use of a technique as a form of treatment for
physical or medical problems without the advice of a physician
either directly or indirectly. The intent of the author is only to
offer information of a general nature to help you in your quest
for emotional and spiritual well-being. In the event you use any
of the information in this book for yourself, which is your right,
the author and the publisher assume no responsibility for your
actions.

Dedicated to my family:

My Soul partner,
husband and friend Jeff
and our darling team,
Abigail, Giana and Freddie,
who put the sparkle in life and
joy in my heart.

And to my dear Bonnie Rose, who is an
inspiration in herself and the best editor
a writer could have. Thank you!

INTRODUCTION

As I sort through the various paragraphs you'll find on the following pages, I'm reminded of the journey their creation has taken me on. Like my other inspirational pick-me-up books, they are a collection of work written for the Spiritually Aware Parenting Facebook page. Unlike the others, the writing of them spanned two and a half years.

Time is a baffling thing and I can't believe how quickly it flies.

Over that time my writing work got consumed with running a full time family health food business. I found myself running, stressed, and sometimes overwhelmed. Although consciously aware of how I was feeling and what I was experiencing, I could only manage to raise my vibration to the point of making the best of a difficult situation, feeling like I couldn't see the forest for the trees.

As homeschoolers, our children were involved with every element of the business too and our family of five had dove into an experience which was originally exciting and quickly turned complicated. However, the Universe will always provide and the experience was one of incredible learning, growing and expansion. I think I was being told to put into practice what I thought I knew. I was doing my time in the trenches, and now find myself better for it.

What I found, during my hairy, stressful, crazy time as a business owner, was the power of intention. My focus for each day, created in the morning or set at night, literally set the tone for how the day went. If I forgot to set one, if I went to bed grumbling and cranky, or even just focused on how tired I was, the following day was set to that dial. When I became aware again, and allowed life to flow, when I showed up to the day, with a clear intention to enjoy it, to see small miracles, to be attentive to my children, to set my priorities, or simply the intention to be Spiritually Aware, then the day went smoother, was more enjoyable and moments of pure joy were discovered by each member of our "team". Hence the title of this book; for often the writing of these passages became an intention for the day for me.

What I've also learnt over the past couple of years, is the importance of letting go of control. I know I don't have all the answers and I know I don't know the best way for things to unfold. I'm on the ride of life and I can decide how I feel in it. I can feel my way through each moment to moment, each choice by choice. But the full picture, *that* can be worked out by the universal manager. We live in a hectic world and the faster things go the more we seem to reach for control, trying to slow life down, *make* it go smoother, *make* it go our way. But the only way to let it go; is to let it go. Taking that moment and then taking it a little longer; Focusing on breathing and then focusing on our Source, our inner being, our souls, our God; Showing up to the day. To live simply and in wonder and setting the intention to be spiritually aware; that's what makes a hectic life a good journey, and full of laughter, love and good moments.

I hope you enjoy *Intentions for the Spiritually Aware Parent*. Its content has helped me, as it always does. There is nothing that gives me greater joy than to show up to a blank page and have my fingers type what I need to hear. Editing them for this book has let me re-read and re-absorb them again, which was again often required reading for my soul.

As with my family, the connection I find in the Facebook community of Spiritually Aware Parenting, as well as you the reader, is a connection of co-creators that I love to create with. I love seeing how SAP has moved and grown over the past few years. What started as simple baby techniques, looking through our children's spiritual eyes, has transcended to finding our own spiritual centers as parents, and shining out.

Keep shining dear readers, I love to feel your rays!

May you feel through your moments and enjoy the bliss of connection each of your days. May love fill your life, laughter fill your house and joy fill your heart.

Be well, happy and thrive always, my friends.

Christina Fletcher

Intentions

For the
Spiritually Aware
Parent

Let's make it our resolution to see our children as the people they really are, no matter what their age or stage they are going through.

Let's promise to cherish and revel in their moments of connection and appreciate their off moments, knowing they will grow and learn from them as they pass. Let's focus on their true spiritual selves, who they are at their core.

At the same time, let's promise to do the same for ourselves, to find the moments to connect, to appreciate, to love, to laugh and to learn.

Let's chose to feel good, because it feels good to feel good, and from the state of feeling better, better things flow in.

Let the truest versions of ourselves shine through and may our days be full of moments of joy, happiness and laughter that we share with our children and all those around us.

We have to let go of the little things to let life flow in with all the wellbeing it has to offer us. So often there's a buildup of things that niggle us, unconsciously dragging us down.

When we find our focus shifting to the things that aren't going well, the things people do that bother us, even a sound from our children's games that grate us the wrong way, we gradually build up resistance to the wellbeing. Sure, sometimes there are big things that feel off to us and we have to work our way through them to find a way to feel better about them, but the little niggles have to be let go and released. For the little things tally up and soon we feel off without knowing the real cause. It can become our default perspective.

Therefore, appreciate what goes well, notice when people we love do well, laugh away the little things, and life becomes open with possibilities, wellbeing ever flowing towards us.

We all have the choice to see life happenings through a perspective that feels better or one that doesn't.

We get to choose our reactions to the things around us. We get to decide how we feel. To offer this truth to our children, to let them be whoever they choose, but to raise them with the knowledge that they do indeed choose, is a parenting choice that gives a sense of freedom.

We are here to protect our children, to offer them the best in life. But we are also here to provide them with options, a chance to see how different things feel, to try them out and decide what feels best to them, what expresses Who They Really Are.

We can't control the outcome of their childhood, but by being true to ourselves, and following our own choices of feeling better, we give them tools to last a lifetime.

We all have things that concern and worry us. We all have things that can make stress rise up within us. We all have problems.

By pretending they don't exist in order to "be positive" we don't convince our deeper selves of anything. Rather, by dodging the topic, we actually give more power to it. The trick is to face the problem and then find a positive way of dealing with it.

It can be the process of offering it up, opening ourselves up to solutions from Source, it can be to find positive aspects of the things that bother us (such as focusing on the wonderful things our children have done in the day, rather than worrying they are disconnected) or we can simply acknowledge the emotion, see it for what it is, and then focus on a better feeling thought, purposely healing the negative space we were in before.

Life is about balance.

So often we see day to day living through our
outer mind, which we use in conversations,
interactions and daily business.
When we stop to see it through our inner mind,
closing our eyes to the world around us and
sinking into that space of quiet within us we see
things from a whole perspective. We can sense our
own spirits/selves with a deeper clarity and when
we open our minds back to the outer view we
retain that sense of self.

It is why we came here to this earth, in these
bodies, to have the balance of the inner and the
outer, the action and the contemplation, the calm
and the excitement, the noise and the quiet.
By offering our children the tools to find this
balance we give them a sense of wholeness and the
ability to shift perspectives in their lives.

Stress is often the first indication of disconnection.

Sometimes stress comes when we have a specific concept of how things should be going, but it's going differently than we want, so we try to hold onto the reigns to steer it in the right direction.

However, often the universe is offering us a new perspective or opportunity, that when we try to control the moment, we block the new thought.

With that block, stress is created, for we have made a disconnection between us and the true spiritual beings we are. However, with stress as the first indication, when we acknowledge it, we can easily change the direction of our sails.

I have, many times, said the wrong thing at the wrong time. Sometimes I have laughed and created an awkward moment, sometimes I have accidentally hurt someone, or gotten carried away with a joke.

Isn't it to be expected that our children will also experience these off moments? And in experiencing them and feeling the offness, isn't that what helps them grow and learn, reaching for the better experience next time?

We are all people, and in the rush of day to day, in the off moments, in the stressed moments, in the tired moments, it is easy to react to life and not do what pleases others.

So is it with our children; And with our understanding of that, and their own experience, we can offer them a supportive hand rather than a glare, a harsh word or a frustrated tone.

In understanding ourselves, we understand our children. In understanding our children, we understand ourselves.

Why do we resist the relief that connecting with our children can bring?

Why do we try to convince ourselves that accomplishing as much as we can, in as small of space as possible, will bring us happiness?

Life is full of hidden gems, moments of connection, laughter and relief if we just trust in them.

When we make the shift to appreciating connecting with our children, talking to them before bed, snuggling up to them that little bit longer, listening to their stories, sharing a laugh or a smile, when we see them as the delightful people they are to spend time with, we can feel ourselves relax and adjust our sails to being the parent we all wish to be: the conscious, present aware person that we all are within.

Sometimes our children feel good exploring things that make them feel scared or sad, like watching scary movies that fill them with excitement, listening to sad music or sad tales that make them want to cry. The thing to remember is that, although we want our children to feel good, to jive and to be happy, it is the exploration of emotion that means they FEEL, and feel strongly.

In this world we live in it is easy to fall into a zone of not feeling, to go about our day to day only being half present. When we feel we are consciously present in that moment. When our children experience negative emotion they FEEL it entirely, and we can help them refocus their thoughts and feeling spaces onto different things which they can also feel strongly about.

It is a true gift to Feel with our whole selves and not have it muted, and being offered tools to decide how we want to feel and how to use stories, music or new thoughts, to shift that feeling space, is the gift of a lifetime.

To have fun with our children doesn't always have to mean setting aside time to play with them. Rather to have fun with them is to enjoy their company, to let the time you share together doing day to day activities be lighthearted and full of laughter.

Yes, it is a wonderful thing to stop and PLAY with our children, it can connect ourselves and our children and change our habitual feeling space, but it is the everyday banter, the sense of connection, of friendship, of consideration and enjoyment of being in each other's presence that creates a happy home and a bond with our children that goes beyond just parenting.

Just as we can view our children as more than just "children", so too can we drop the pretense of being just "parents" and be Who we really are in the company of our darlings.

Sometimes our children feel off and they try to gain control by wanting the power of the scenario. As parents our automatic reaction can be to gain the power back and take control, however in doing so we create a ball game, with the power being sought for and everyone losing.

When we see "power" becoming the goal (either by our children or ourselves) it's alright to take a step back and talk about working together for common goals. We all want our children to thrive individually. We love to see them know their own minds and stand up for their own beliefs. However, it's alright to point out the difference of what serves a person individually and what serves the group as the whole.

That is why I love the analogy of an orchestra, as parents we aren't the controllers, merely the conductors. We know that each player can play beautifully on their own, and their song is perfect, but a conductor makes sure that when played together everyone works as a whole, making a perfect chorus. Each player can then go off alone and play their own song.

Each moment, each instance, we have a choice of how to react or how to act.

Being Spiritually Aware is about being conscious of that choice at each moment and how to be true to our deeper selves as much as possible.

We all react badly sometimes, we will all at one time or another react from stress, frustration or upset. However, when we are aware of it, when we can sense it rising within us, we can remind ourselves to act from a place of love.

Sometimes it is logical to be angry, sometimes frustration seems like the only path to take, yet when we choose to see through the eyes of love and choose the most loving action we open our hearts and minds to different options and other doors always open up to let the sun shine in.

It is by being the best version of ourselves that we offer the best example for our children.

So often we put aside making the slight adjustments to ourselves, even though when we make them we feel better. Sometimes it is easier to sit and watch a television show than to find the space to go within and "Be", sometimes we think it's easier to react and be angry at those who hurt us, rather than going within and acting from a place of love. Sometimes it seems easier to fall into a torrent of negative thoughts, letting ourselves spiral into feeling overwhelmed, rather than shifting gears and looking for positive aspects or ways to find relief.

However, each time we rise above the "easy" option and choose to take the "aware" one, each time we choose the better feeling path, we not only empower our children to do the same, we also find that it was no more effort than it is for water to roll over a stone in a stream.

Families are made up of individuals, however we are inter-connected in a way that often goes unrealized.

As a close knit unit a family bounces off each other creating an energy made up of the feeling spaces of those within it.

We react off of each other and literally bounce off.

When we notice a child is feeling off, however easy it is to react with upset and possibly frustration, by seeing it as a reaction within the unit we can focus in on what we ourselves are emitting.

Love, understanding, appreciation and resetting the tone of the house can often throw the needed ingredient in the mix and a child can connect again, whereas frustration and upset can just add more to the imbalance.

Be a tone setter and take an inner moment to connect to your truest self. For there's no point asking from others what we can't do ourselves.

We all know what it feels like to only be half listened to, or to be talked at, rather than to. We know what it's like to feel as though we're in the way or holding someone up. We all know what it's like to feel that our opinions don't matter.

When we forget to see our children, no matter how young, as the people they really are, with their own thoughts, opinions and feelings, which may differ from our own, but are no less valuable, then we're like a brick wall that can't be surmounted. It can be a very desolate place.

What many parents don't realize is that it's a lonely place for both of us, as when we cut ourselves off from those we love, we are alone on the other side, running the cycle of day to day living without the company of someone who can offer us fun, laughter, joy, pride as well as suggestions and different perspectives.

Although the reflection is different than it was, we are the same people who look in the mirror now as we were when we were children.

We see through the same eyes as we did then, we think in the same voice, feel with the same heart.

It is the deeper sense of ourselves that we must act from, the sense of truth that we must foster, rather than who the image reflects.

Same too, as we view our children, it is important to see their own essence as who they really are, which is eternal, rather than the image that is reflected to us which is ever changing as they grow.

How we see our children doesn't just effect how they are but our reactions to them.

When we see them as the pure, positive spirits they really are at their core, and as people, who occasionally make mistakes, we can act from a place of love and understanding.

After all, we all make mistakes sometimes.

When we see them as "children" who do things we don't want them to do, who possibly get in the way, or make messes which make things difficult for us, we see them as an excuse to feel bad ourselves and react from anger and frustration.

Our children are growing Beings, and so are we. We may be on different parts of the journey, but the journey is the same.

Our negative emotions give us resounding indicators of the inner work we need to do, if we only stop for a moment to observe them rather than react from them.

Just as our small children hate the feeling of being "off" in a day and melt down into a tantrum, so too do we often get caught up in feeling off, blame everything under the sun, look to others as the cause and fall into the trap of being grouchy, irritable or easily angered.

When we get into the habit of observing how we feel, we can sense feeling off, and look for ways to feel better. Sometimes it means banging around a scenario to find the relief giving solution, often it means distracting our attention onto something, like playing with our children, until we feel better and can then go back to the problem.

Sometimes, usually in fact, we can reset our course, by going within, focusing on our breath, lifting our eyes to the sky and trusting that wellbeing flows for us.

Oh, the cycle that is created when we have "off" days the same days that our children feel "off".

It is so easy to think we need them to connect first, in order for our connection to get started. However, no matter how tempting it is to talk, fix and correct our children's moment into connection, it is going within ourselves, that the cycle is broken.

When we distract our children with something fun for just a moment, so we can collect our thoughts and return to the blissful feeling of being our truest selves, then we allow the space for the day to move into a different direction.

There are always times when our children have issues with going to sleep, let's face it, we've all had problems getting to sleep at one time or another.

When a child is restless it is a sign of them feeling stressed and agitated, therefore no matter how upsetting it may be for us, adding more stress into the equation just makes the matter worse. It is, rather, a question of tapping into what the feeling space of the home is at the moment and relaxing into shifting the focus ourselves.

When we make it our own process to relax and let life flow as it should, then our children can adjust to that feeling space and relax themselves, drifting into a peaceful slumber knowing that all is well.

By the time a child is a certain age they need some "drop time" to tap into themselves and retreat from the chaos of the day or their own chattering minds.

Often this comes naturally as we see our children drift into imaginary worlds in their play or in their thoughts, or as they get older and their showers get longer or they sleep in later, it is their spirit's way of calling them back to connection. Yet how often do we get caught up in our own chaos in our days and fall into the trap of insisting our children don't take the "drop times"? When we are rushing around it is so easy to tell our children to snap out of their imaginary wanderings, or to hurry up in the bathroom.

Yet, when we remember that they are taking connection time, when we remember that those distant looks we sometimes get aren't always about not listening to us, it's often a calling to connection, we would do well to encourage it. Otherwise we encourage them to keep running, never stopping and finding no peace of mind.

As parents we are often haunted by making the "right" decision.

From the moment we get pregnant until the moment our children are grown and live independently we find ourselves constantly throwing different options into the mix and trying to figure out which path to take for the "good of our child". So often in deciding what is best, we focus on an unforeseeable future, trying to guess where each road leads. The only way to truly feel our way to a decision is to stop logically breaking it down, guessing how our children will react and do what feels right in the moment.

What creates the best now? What provides the best tools now, so that they can use them to launch into the next New choice? What is your heart encouraging you to do? What feels like the most Yourself? When we chose what feels best, we set ourselves free for the future. For no matter what, when we can look into the mirror and say we did what felt right to our hearts, it is hard to find anything to regret.

Our children naturally get embarrassed when they do something they shouldn't and we ask them to stop. This can often result in two choices, one they can simply grow quiet, letting it fester inside of them or they can flush out the action, and start acting goofy or over the top. No matter what, insecurity, uncertainty and embarrassment are sure to follow, when we say no to something they were doing.

It's not necessarily a bad thing, as it's simply contrast to feeling good and part of the growing process, but how we act is fundamental to keeping it healthy. By offering reason when we ask them to stop something, and then making it light and fun rather than heavy, we can keep the moment flowing past and onto the next moment of fun. Also, by understanding the feeling of embarrassment and insecurity, which we have all felt from time to time, we can see the world through their eyes, tell them we understand how they feel and relate to it, and create a gentle growing experience, where mistakes are honored for what they teach and seen as important milestones.

Questions... often it seems that our children can ask so many questions. It's easy to fall into the trap of brushing them off, avoiding connecting with them in discussion and in giving the answers they are looking for. But what our children understand, and we often forget, is that asking questions, seeking the meaning or deeper meaning in everything, from the ground up, is what helps us all grow. Questions dig deep and from them we can learn about other people, the world around us, and even ourselves.

When we start asking questions to our children we open a door for them which leads to self confidence and a feeling of connection. What they have to say matters and they can offer insight that others can't see.

Therefore, we should ask our children about things, ask them if they've seen our lost keys and how their days went. We need to embrace their questions too, fulfilling their need for information and curiosity. Together, by asking and answering questions, we can spark new life into our family, learning about each other and creating a harmony of healthy, sincere, curiosity.

Life, with all its changes, even weather changes, can be overwhelming for children. The atmosphere changes, the energy in the air. Parents get busy doing different things, new things. It's easy to feel left behind, frustrated and confused.

Often, as parents, we think our children are going through whiny, clingy phases. We blame it on their age, being overtired or hungry. However, it is through seeing life through their eyes, taking the moment to imagine how it feels to be them, that we can meet their needs and make their transitions with change more comfortable. Children live in the Now always and when changes come and their Now feels different it can be a bumpy road, but by making it fun and sometimes sitting with them bathed in a sense of security and love, they can face whatever changes each day brings.

The intermingling of human beings, who are all positive spiritual beings in human form, can be a complicated blend of energy, feelings, and situations. When we are stressed with others it helps to focus on their truest essence, rather than what they are presenting to us at the moment. Often we sum up a person as what they do, what they say and how they stumble around grumbling, when we don't know the instances that have got them to that point.

It can consume us and affect our feeling space more than theirs. Therefore, when we shift our focus to their highest selves, seeing them as Who They Really Are, who might be making mistakes, learning the hard way, feeling off in order to have the bliss of getting on track again, figuring it out, defining themselves, in the process, getting caught up in the small stuff and simply being in a different space than us at that current moment, we can feel so much better and offer them a space of feeling more like themselves, rather than keeping them in the space of feeling Off by always seeing them as that.

Life is about balance.

So often we see day to day living through our outer mind, which we use in conversations, interactions and daily business.

When we stop to see it through our inner mind, closing our eyes to the world around us and sinking into that space of quiet within us we see things from a whole perspective.

We can sense our own spirits/selves with a deeper clarity and when we open our minds back to the outer view we retain that sense of self. It is why we came here to this earth, in these bodies, to have the balance of the inner and the outer, the action and the contemplation, the calm and the excitement, the noise and the quiet.

By offering our children the tools to find this balance we give them a sense of wholeness and the ability to shift perspectives in their lives.

The intermingling of human beings, who are all positive spiritual beings in human form, can be a complicated blend of energy, feelings, and situations. When we are stressed with others it helps to focus on their truest essence, rather than what they are presenting to us at the moment.

Often we sum up a person as what they do, what they say and how they stumble around grumbling, when we don't know the instances that have got them to that point. It can consume us and affect our feeling space more than theirs.

Therefore, when we shift our focus to their highest selves, seeing them as Who They Really Are, who might be making mistakes, learning the hard way, feeling off in order to have the bliss of getting on track again, figuring it out, defining themselves, in the process, getting caught up in the small stuff and simply being in a different space than us at that current moment, we can feel so much better and offer them a space of feeling more like themselves, rather than keeping them in the space of feeling Off by always seeing them as that.

We can only work with what we've got.

When a day is going haywire and everything we try seems to just build up to negative results sometimes we can try to feel better by imagining, visualizing improved circumstances (if only it was sunny, if only we were somewhere else, if only they would have a nap, things would be better if she would just play alone for a moment. Etc). However, this process can actually make the day go from bad to worse, as we are actually putting the stress on what we don't have and why the moment is going so badly.

When we stop in our tracks, play with our children, throw caution to the wind and leave the dishes in the sink, we can refocus on to the things that are going well in each moment. We can flush out what we appreciate and take the time to really appreciate it.

The old "grass is always greener" saying may be cliché, but it's also a habit of thought we can take part in way too often. The grass is green wherever we go, it only takes a moment to look around ourselves and see the beauty in it.

If a child is acting from a sped up space, being over excited, hyper, and dancing in circles, by offering them calming programs to watch, sitting with them to read a book, singing calm, slower songs, providing some focused play like blocks or simply talking in a slower, calmer way and engaging in conversation, we provide the opposite so they know what it feels like and we break the cycle rather than speeding ourselves up so we can meet them in that space.

We can set the tone of the house by providing the feeling space we wish to see.

Same too if we feel the house is lacking in energy, by being positive and enthusiastic ourselves we can lift our family's space. The trick is to feel what we wish to feel authentically, for our children will know if it's sincere.

In our intention to go within and connect
so we can be the best version of ourselves
for our children, we often forget that our
children can provide the best opportunities
for us to connect and be just that.

Relax, play, chatter, have fun and enjoy
each moment: for they chose us to be with
them at this time and in the great scheme
of everything, this is just where we are all
meant to be.

There is great relief in the freedom of being a spiritually aware parent, for the word *aware* allows us all to have bad days, off days and slip ups.

It is in being aware of what our frustration and stress indicates, feeling the off moments and adjusting how we feel that helps us grow from our mistakes.

Spiritually Aware Parenting acknowledges that we are all on a journey, growing and learning. Each off day sparks new solutions and new desires. Each mistake and problem clarifies what we want and Who we are.

With that knowledge, we can see our children through the same light, as on a spiritual journey, feeling off, having bad days, and learning, growing and defining themselves.

The connection is never turned off from us, rather it is us who gets slightly unaligned from our own connection to Source.

It is like a Wireless internet Connection, once we readjust our position we get the signal clean and clear. It takes little effort, no work and simply stopping in our tracks for a few seconds to go within and breathe.

To stop in our tracks, look up to the sky and let a sense of awe settle in within us.

To stop in a moment, to observe our life, rather than get caught up in it, and let love pour over us.

A few seconds can bring connection back, but it then can shift a whole day around.

We are forever learning and defining ourselves on this journey of life, starting from before we even take that first breath.

We gather experiences as we go, we make mistakes, we have off days and then connected ones, when things flow with ease and wonderment.

From all of this, we take what we love, what feels good, what feels right, as well as, what feels wrong, off and causes us discomfort. With this knowledge, we make new choices, new decisions, new roads of discovery.

What a perspective to see our babes in arms, as they start off on their path. What a view to appreciate our children's off moments or their excited moments of discovery.

And what a comfort for us, as we continue, improving each day, defining each moment, feeling our way towards the best version of ourselves.

We can all form bad habits, but when our children do, often, we see it as a statement of Who They Are, rather than something they have simply slipped into.

Being too rough with their siblings or friends, certain tones of voice, or even being critical or negative, are all things that we can get into the habit of as, within the world, we are around them every day. We can be influenced by television, advertisements, internet, even strangers in the grocery store.

When our children suddenly have a negative reaction to things, by assuming it as a habit, rather than a choice they have made, we can bring it to their attention and ask them to leave it aside for a bit, giving them the opportunity to be aware of it, break the habit, and, if they want, bring it back into their lives if they choose.

When we are aware of being caught up in negative experiences, we can all back track and truly decide how we want to be.

It is worthwhile to question our own connection when we feel our children are acting from a place of Offness.

Often, while we worry and fret that our children are disconnected and not acting in harmony with the rest of the house, when we turn our focus to ourselves we sometimes find that perhaps we aren't ringing out with the same tune as well.

Sometimes our children's behavior is simply an indicator, a reaction, to the mental and emotional space we've been in ourselves. As a family, we are always bouncing off each other and before we try to judge how well one member of the family is doing we need to always tune in to ourselves to make sure we are jiving first.

To practice "Baby led" or "child led" parenting, letting our children take the lead and show when they are ready for their next expansion, is a promising practice of listening and being conscious parent.

However, the parent/child relationship is a co-created one. Although "Parent led" suggests control and demands, there is the element of "instinct led." Sometimes, our children can be in a habitual grove and suddenly something feels off to us.

When we feel that offness rise up inside of us, it is right to slowly shift direction, even for our children. It doesn't have to be forced, or unpleasant, rather introducing new thoughts, ideas or processes.

When we follow our instincts for change, the outcome is usually quite smooth, however, if we are being an "instinct-led" family, than it is only balanced by trusting our children's instincts as well.

We all have an ideal vision of our home and family. We all wish for it to ring out with laughter, kindness and good will, and we reach that ideal version now and again.

As with individual spirits, a family of spirits will reach its best version, experience contrast and then learn from it, constantly improving itself and growing together.

A family is not a static thing like an image on the wall, rather it is fluid, growing and expressing itself as the people within it define themselves.

An ideal version provides us with what we want to feel like, but there is no room for judgment when we don't reach it, for when we judge what we see, we hold ourselves back from the learning we can do from where we are, from the growing we need to experience in order to reach new heights.

Our chattering brains and fragmented minds can convince us that we have no time to stop and be; we have to keep going.

However, when we take a few moments to stop, focus on our breathing, relax and be in our moment completely, we gather our thoughts from ever fragmented corner and become who we are in that conscious moment with one pure signal.

In our fragmented space we can feel like we have to control the connection points of our children, and find ways to help them connect.

However, when we take control of our chattering brains, when we stop and simply "be" for a moment, we offer our children a tool by example, which they will understand the workings of, simply by the energy we emanate.

Change has to be made from the inside out.

We can spend our time seeing things in our lives that we wish would be changed, we can stress and fret about trying to change them, but in fact their existence is actually a result of where we are within ourselves.

When we go within and allow life to flow over and past us, when we return to our days, the solutions come, life takes a shift and all becomes well again, bouncing off of our new perspective.

Life is ever flowing and although sometimes day in day out life can feel the same, with the same routine and habits, in fact, shift after shift, life is ever changing.

We grow, we learn, we expand, our children do the same.

Just as our skin sheds layers and creates new ones over time without our noticing, so life does.

Each day is a new day, full of infinite possibilities, so long as we let them flow in and through us.

Being Spiritually Aware can work or BE work. We brush our teeth every day, we eat, comb our hair and answer the phone habitually, but so often we see taking the time to be spiritually aware as a break from routine, a time to relax, that we often can't afford to take.

It becomes a chore, work, as we struggle to find peace of mind amidst the chaos.

When we take five minutes to have a spiritual check in, just as we would have a shower or any other natural self care moment, the benefits show up instantaneously. When we stop in our tracks to see how we feel, when we make the adjustments we need by simply refocusing on that which goes well in our days, life flows and spirit does the work for us.

You are here to be YOU.

Being a parent is an aspect of you, but it doesn't define you, at any rate.

In fact, we define our parenting by being ourselves and that is precisely why our children chose us, because of Who We Are, not because of how down pat we've got the parenting thing.

By being true to ourselves, taking the time to tap into our inner natures, to work out who we really are and not what people expect us to be, we can offer our children the fullest version of that.

We can also live our life purpose, to experience life as Who We Really Are, full of joy, love, laughter and conscious moments.

Our ideas of how a perfect life should be is often
not what a perfect life is.

We can plan, we can ponder and we can
contemplate, we can visualize perfect outcomes
and as long as they make us feel good in the
moment, as long as they can lift our hearts, it has
served us well.

But no matter how many times life throws a
spoke in our wheels and sends our plans spinning
out of control, Life IS perfect.

It is our perspective of the chaos, how we embrace
the difficult times as the launching places they
are, that define ourselves and the moments that
follow. There are always mysterious elements at
work, taking the wheel from us when we get off
course without knowing. Things are always lined
up so we can get the most out of life and define
ourselves more.

Strive to feel good or at least better in the
moment, and the moments line up to create that
perfect life we dream of.

When we are irritated and stressed we can get into a rut of trying to find connection.

We stay in the position of being frustrated, but look for a positive place from there.

We try to pivot around the situation, try to make ourselves feel better, all the while focused on what's bothering us and from there, connection can't be found.

Take a moment break from problems.

It is only when we stop ourselves in our tracks, and stop "trying" to connect, that we can connect. It is when we close our eyes and float for a moment, when we stop on the street to stare at the sky, when we fully appreciate our children and savor that appreciation with all our being, using it as a distraction for better moments, that we can finally drop into the place of connection to Who We Really Are.

Life and connection are meant to flow easily, therefore, whenever we are stressed we would do well to stop, breathe, laugh, love, appreciate and relax into the very moment we are in.

Our children will become passionate about things
we know nothing about.

Our children's hearts will skip a beat over
something that may leave us confused.

Our children will be on the leading edge of
technology while we're still figuring out touch
screen. Our children will learn past what we know
and exceed our expectations by reaching heights
that at this moment we can't even imagine.

We spend so much effort trying to think what is
best for our children, when really by providing
them with the foundational tools of following
THEIR heart, feeling positive about themselves
and their days and how to connect to the source
within THEM and then setting them up in a field
of infinite possibilities, they will create a
wonderful life, the life they came to live.

Life is a journey, unfolding as it goes and while
anything is possible for our children, so too, is
anything possible for us.

However tempting it is to fall into the trap of thinking life would be best if we all agreed and saw things the same way, the world is a wonderful space created for the diversity of it all.

It's an important thing to remind ourselves, as we raise our children, passing on the perspective of diversity allows them to, not only be accepting of others, but be true to themselves, to listen to their own inner music, to use their perspectives and make-up, as a statement of Who They Are.

It also allows them to see us as people, people who are constantly growing, learning and playing, just like them, only differently.

By exposing our children to variety, but respecting other people's differences, by agreeing to disagree with our family members and friends and by having a foundation of love not fear, we pass on to our children the ability to have open hearts and minds and to be true to everything they are.

Whenever we feel disconnected from our children it can feel like we are banging our heads against an invisible wall trying to understand how they are feeling, where they are coming from, and who they are.

However, at our deepest core we are connected to them in a way that defies intellect.

A great practice to get into is to spend some time observing life through our children's eyes. Before bed, or at a quiet moment, it is relieving to simply allow yourself to drift into your child's world, reminding yourself of who they REALLY are, and getting a sense of where they are now emotionally, spiritually and mentally.

Just as we would close our eyes and tap into our babies' essences before they were born, getting a sense of who they were then, so now can we tap into that deep connection and get a sense of who they are now.

The days that follow are often filled with connected moments of understanding as we've adjusted ourselves to our children getting older day by day.

Everything happens at the right time and in the perfect way.

Although it's easy to fall into the fear based perspective that our children SHOULD be doing things at certain ages and in certain ways, when they are ready, it miraculously unfolds in a way that expresses everything about their true selves.

We can spend our children's younger years frustrated and anxious that they don't help out enough, but then they hit a point that helping comes organically through them and they are happy to lend a hand.

We can worry they don't know about certain things, but then life opens up and it is the perfect opportunity to discuss it with them.

When we trust that all unfolds just as it should we can stop and enjoy the journey and each stepping stone our children land on, at each stop along the way.

Each moment has the seed of a new beginning in it and by giving it intention and attention we let that new life spring forth.

Our children know this, and while we worry and plan, and contemplate the consequences of all they do, they know within their being that life is full of reset buttons, new chances and new experiences. They know that if they feel off and all is going wrong, they can stop in their moment to start again.

We can get so caught up in the details of life we dig ourselves an emotional hole we find difficult to get out of. We feel we have to run the gamut, complete the course and slowly work through things, forgetting that we simply cement ourselves more in place when we focus on what is bothering us.

There is a reset button, there are always new beginnings, sometimes like a small seed springing forth, barely reaching the top of the soil, the new beginning is a small shift or movement in perspective, but it grows and each new beginning has the potential to reach great heights.

There's no reason for us to beat ourselves up for having an off day, for off days are the launching points for the new version of ON!

When we seem to be on a run of reacting rather than acting, talking in tones that feel unlike who we are, or who we want to be, when we seem to drop everything and get frustrated easily, it's important to simply recognize the moment and see it for what it is.

The world won't end for it and our children won't suffer for it, provided we treat it with the honesty it deserves and then take a new direction of perspective.

We should always remind ourselves, each off moment is a doorway to a new adventure, it's a learning curve, a decision, a choice, and when we choose we want to feel better, and shift focus to the things that get us there, even if it means cutting the course of the Off day short, we will find ourselves in a mental and emotional space which feels new and wonderful, thankful for the offness that launched us there.

There is a wonderful sense of new discovery and excitement when we revel in the things our children like and do differently than us.

So often we want to encourage our children to try the things we've liked or agree with the way we see things, but it often backfires and our children push against it.

When we simply offer them a buffet of choices and samples in life and then sit back to watch them grow, learn and define themselves, we can learn so much about ourselves and the world around us.

We can't limit our children with our own limitations, or even within our own perspectives, rather we have to trust that we are providing what we can and with their perspectives and discernment they can then express themselves as everything they really are.

We all have moments when we put our heads on the table and sigh "I can't stand it".

We've experienced frustration, upset, disappointment and all negative emotion from different perspectives and situations.

Therefore, it should be with understanding that we comfort our children when they experience the same.

From the moment we can't do something we want to, we can feel frustration, and our reactions to the feeling changes and progresses through life, as different things lead us there, but the emotion is still the same.

Therefore, we can offer hugs, comfort, distraction, even chocolate, but it's through understanding that we remind our children that negative emotion is part of the human journey which we all experience.

It is how we deal with it that matters and that is part of the journey too.

As parents we often watch our children with a skeptical eye, as we can feel like their behavior reflects how we are doing as parents.

However, we would do better to look for the things that they are doing well and focus on that.

They have off moments and connected ones and we are not in charge of either, rather by seeing the things that they thrive on, by taking part in their joyful moments, by observing their processes as they learn, grow, and expand, we notice the tools we are passing down to them or get inspired to offer different ones.

We are not in charge of their journey, only here to offer them a helping hand and the tools to create a happy life.

That is parenting we can feel secure in.

As parents, we can go within and spend time with our inner beings, but we have a tie to the physical reality of it all, keeping an ear out for our children's call.

Although this can be seen as a hindrance, it is in fact an opportunity.

Our children provide us with the chance to bring our inner worlds into the moment, rather than the tempting habit of closing them off until everyone has grown up.

As parents, we are at a time to find the bliss in each flower, sunset, and gentle breeze.

We are in the place of tuning ourselves to the vibrational realities of the world and savoring its music.

Trying to sit in a state of prayer or meditation for 20 minutes might have a parent feeling incompetent or simply be impossible, but to see the divine in the every day, to play with our darlings with full consciousness, to find cause to laugh, smile, and sigh authentically to our core, is a spiritual state that parents can relax into.

And in that relaxation we truly tap into everything we really are.

We've all heard the phrase "when it rains, it pours" and we all know the feeling of things piling up, as we race faster and faster for the finish line that doesn't exist.

When things seem to be cramming us in and we can feel the tension rising, the most important thing to do, and probably one of the hardest at that time, is to relax and shift focus to something that relieves our worried minds and hearts.

Our children provide the best opportunities for this as they are always willing to take part in something fun or to play with us.

The world also provides us many chances to shift, taking in a sunset, watching the birds fly above us, or simply admiring the leaves as they spring back to life on the trees.

When we shift focus from the "pouring rain", we set into motion the magic of the law of attraction, and the feeling of relief will start "piling up", rather than holding up the magnet of stress that started the race in the first place.

When our children are acting unlike themselves and we sense them stressed and feeling off then it's easy to want to help them feel better. However, the only real thing we can do is provide them the tools to help them connect again.

It's impossible to make connection happen for anyone else but ourselves. When we find our own inner connection and talk about the process we take to find it, when we offer our children opportunities to find quiet time within, even through art, writing or nature walks, when we bring up what we appreciate and spark dialogue about things we love, when we play, connect together and laugh, we open a window for our children when they might feel the doors are closed.

It is always up to them to connect with their truest selves, but we can offer a hand to help them get there, holding the vision of Who they are deep within our hearts and minds making the trip easier to finding it for themselves.

Life happens and however easy it is to want to create the "perfect" life, it is through our reactions and actions to the life in front of us that creates the life we live.

When we feel stressed or overwhelmed, however tempting it is to look upon the problems, or the life that is less than perfect, that simply creates more of the same and more stress will pile up.

It is only by taking a step away from the problem, giving our full focus to something that brings us joy, to playing with our children or simply savoring a moment of peace and finding wellbeing again, that we can return to the scenario with renewed clarity. By taking charge of how we feel at each overwhelming "off" moment and choosing our reaction we create days that represent Who We Are and decide Who we Want to Be.

There is a fundamental difference between

finding time to go within,

telling ourselves to go within,

thinking about going within

and actually Going Within.

So often we see the moment to steal some connection time, but within those brief moments we tell ourselves to become still and calm life down. Calming life down and becoming still is done by sinking in the moment and not through planning to do it.

It is by letting our minds shift focus to the beauty around us or the things we appreciate, rather than TELLING our minds to shift focus. Going within, tapping in and turning on is an act of focus rather than a thought to think. When we learn how to shift focus and let go of the stress of the day (and use our moments wisely) we truly choose how we feel.

Everything happens at the right moment, at the right time.

When we trust in the process of the moment we can let go of the little things that seem to be missed, or things we feel should be learnt or understood.

When we trust in the right time, we can let go of the future and shift focus to creating the best moment, rather than achieve our plans or goals all at once.

Breathe and relax, enjoying the day, creating the most for each moment.

When life speeds up, and we find ourselves with lots of things to do and to get done, it's easy to enter a zone; a place where we just speed along, forgetting who we are and reacting from that point.

When we are spiritually aware, or at least have signed up to be, although we can feel ourselves enter the zone we also have red warning lights pop up to signal us to find a moment to reconnect. These indicators can come in the form of feeling extra tired, noticing the focus shifting to negative outcomes, even the rising feeling within ourselves of negative mind chatter or the temptation to just lose it.

When life hits that point the trick is to tap in to ourselves and to stop the chatter of looking out into the world or the future.

To seize a moment to breathe, appreciate and trust until we feel like ourselves again.

When we go back into the speeding moments of our lives our inner resources will be replenished and all will roll merrily along again.

Just as we have traffic signs on the road to tell us to slow down or stop all together, so too do we have indicators within us to tell us to shift gears, or lanes and refocus our attention.

The indicators can come in all manner of ways, from emotionally, with frustration, stress, depression or anger to more physical responses, such as over-tiredness or sickness.

When we train ourselves to notice the indicators then we can see them as the roadmap they really are. We can follow the signs, slowing down when needed or shifting gears so that we can refocus on things that feel better.

Sometimes we can feel lost, confused by the hectic traffic that goes on in our own heads, but by taking the simple step to remind ourselves to watch how we feel and listen to the signs given to us, we can take a detour to a smoother, happier journey.

Often we can be worried about how our children will react to things in the future or how things will affect them on the whole.

However, worry is still based in the future and our children know that life is created by living in the moment.

Therefore, when we focus on the moment at hand, play with them, smile with them, laugh with them, and create a feeling space of wellbeing and joy, then the future will unfold as it may.

Our children will be able to greet it with a sense of understanding and adjust from the perspective of wellbeing and once the change or stress has past we can all look back at the event and it will feel like a slight bump in the road, rather than the catastrophe we had imagined.

We can plan and give careful thought to the sort of parents we want to be and what we want to pass on to our children.

We can think up games, things to tell them, important information to pass on to them and when the time comes it can end up feeling contrived and un-natural, leaving us feeling like we've let our ideal down.

However, it is an exciting thing to have the desire to pass certain things on and then letting the right time and the right process unfold in the perfect way.

When we trust in our inner desire and universal powers to deliver, suddenly the right words come out, the right opportunities, the perfect game.

We don't have to plan, just trust in our own connection and the universal flow of wellbeing that always delivers. All is well.

When we take a step back to look at our thoughts it's incredible to see how they can create our perspective of our day.

By thinking something is going terribly wrong, even for a few minutes, we can build upon the theme within our thoughts and soon be stressed that nothing can go right.

However, the same can go for positive thoughts as well. When we take a step back and focus on what is going well, and the joy that the people in our lives can bring, when we shift to remind ourselves of every good aspect of the day, we can find thoughts that back that up and soon feel relief regarding each situation.

Our thoughts are powerful things, and although there will always be things to worry and concern ourselves with, we should be careful of the power we place behind them and make sure we balance our thought processes by purposely spending some time creating a beautiful space within our own minds, therefore creating beautiful days.

There will always be times when things aren't going quite how you wish they would.

Children go to bed later than you wanted, the house isn't ringing with the tones of joy and light quite how you would like, your own dealings with stresses and reactions don't feel quite like the highest version of yourself.
At these times, it's important to remind ourselves that life is a journey, a process, of one transition to another.
There is no set way in how our families function, rather only how our families grow.
By acknowledging the things that feel off, we can launch to the solutions to making them feel better. The off moments aren't set in stone, just as the perfect ones aren't either.
All will be well and all continually moves to another connected time.
On and Off, Connected and Disconnected, it is the balanced dance we all partake in, and by doing so we grow, discern and learn.

Life will always throw challenges into the works and as we face them beside our children it is important to be aware of how we feel.

So often within those challenges we can feel stressed, worried, upset and disconnected, and by being honest about how we feel we can be honest with our children and see the situation clearer.

Trust in Love always and watch for the fear that sneaks up upon us.

Things are always well, going precisely as they should on a deeper level.

We are all Spiritual, positive beings and each challenge provides us with what we need. By trusting in Love we can offer love and a feeling of security to our children, no matter how insane life may look from a more worldly perspective.

Often, our perspective of life can shift things from being stressful to joyful.

When we change the story we are telling ourselves about the moments in our life, suddenly we can feel the relief we crave for.

It can be as simple as being stressed about our children's bedtimes to appreciating the game they are in the middle of playing, as basic as seeing our loved ones as having off moments rather than criticizing them in our heads, or allowing ourselves to have off moments too, rather than going down the road of feeling taken advantage of or under appreciated.

There is always a kinder, relieving story to tell and when we choose to feel better, we can feel better and when we feel better, life unfolds in a more relieving way.

Often we can focus on the lack of something in our lives, the lack of time to play, the lack of a chance for a moment to connect, a lack of quiet, when, if we shifted focus, we could use that moment to have what we are convinced we lack.

When we are pondering how we need time to laugh and play, we could be laughing and playing, when we are focused on how we need a moment to relax and tap into our higher selves we can choose to shift focus to our breath and relax.

What we put our minds on and the perspective we adopt is truly our choice and we can seize any moment to change direction of our thoughts. There is no "too late" or "too tired" to feel good, rather there is only the choice to return to the path of Who We Really Are or wait for another moment.

It is always within our grasp.

When we get stressed and overwhelmed, feeling that tension rising within us or feeling overtired, it is often a signal to let go of the control we are trying to gain.

As a parent it is easy to feel we have to have everything under thumb, setting up games and activities, making sure everyone is fed on time and in bed as soon as possible, it can also spread to trying to get others to do what we need them to do in order to have everything in the palm of our hands. However, as a family, it's important to know when it is time to let go of the reins.

Sometimes it's simply relaxing in the moment and letting the chips fall as they may which creates a space for everyone to pick up where we left off. Children find their own amusements and are excited by it, fun and play follows and basic needs seem to be met simply by flowing in.

Trusting in the "universal manager" sometimes allows the space for the stress to simply fall away.

It never fails to amaze me how fast the Universe works when we let it.

When we want something, be it even a moment of relief, an inspiring conversation, or a playtime with our children, when we don't force it or try to control it, if we just let it flow in and trust that it will appear, it always does, even with just moments of our releasing it.

It is the faith in seeing what we want, acknowledging what we don't want, and then simply offering it up to the force of life that gives room to it being realized.

Often we feel that life is less than ideal.

We may not have the time we wish to have with our children, we may feel more rushed than we wish and we wonder how it affects our darling ones who have chosen us to be their parents.

The key is to remember that they did indeed choose us, and in that choosing they knew of our journeys, our obstacles and what we were capable of doing during their childhood years.

We all can only do our best and by trying to be present in the moments we have with our children, by being true to ourselves and tapping in to that deeper source that is forever within and around us, we provide them with what they chose us for.

We are all on a journey together with our children, creating a family unit and days which equal a life, a childhood/parenthood experience. Together we create just what we need.

Life is about balance and we can see that balance all around us.

The balance between light and dark, night and day, hot and cold, on and off... inner and outer. We all need to find that balance in ourselves and often the pendulum can swing either way.

When we live fully in our outer minds, we can often wear out, using our resources and often feeling unlike ourselves, giving ourselves away. When we retreat too far into the inner mind, we can feel cut off from the beauty and wonderful world we live in.

By taking the time to find that inner time, and tapping into that inner self, we can find the balance that creates a wonderful outer life.

The Inner magic spreads wide throughout the outer world.

None of us can jump from feeling overwhelmed or overexcited to calm and joyful, the steps between the two have to be taken.

Therefore, it's unfair to expect our children to be able to go from adrenaline filled, playfulness to calm, peaceful, happy play.

At the right time, it's a question of distracting our children with appreciation of things around them, focused talk, interesting questions and engagement in thoughtful conversation.

Fast paced energy is contagious and we can often get stressed as our children speed up, therefore, our own awareness to how things feel can make life a joyful roller coaster of fast paced excitement, to grounded connection, rather than out of control craziness that can send a household spiraling.

Call yourself back into the moment and simply
Be.

So often we criticize ourselves for not taking
enough time to be present in the moment,
forgetting that we are using up the precious
moment by criticizing.

We let our minds chatter about our chatter heads,
we run around creating to do lists so we have less
to do. When we stop, trust the process of the day
and seize the moment, we take control of our
thoughts and days and instantly feel better
simply by letting the moment wash over us and
living it within its entirety.

We can offer spiritual awareness to our children by creating opportunities for them to be aware of how they feel and shift their own focus.

When they are over stimulated and heading into a hectic space, we can offer them ideas and games to calm down with or exercises like lists of appreciation or visualization to make themselves feel better.

We all get to choose what we think about and what trigger our emotions, we all get to create the default feeling we carry around with us all day long.

By bringing our children's attention to how they feel and how they want to feel, we offer tools to last a lifetime.

There are so many things to appreciate in a parent's life and by appreciating them we rewrite the negative chatter that can fill our heads from time to time.

Appreciation uplifts our hearts and minds to shift to a positive perspective, which can then light upon all elements of our lives.

By appreciating our children's moments of flourishing independence, we shift to seeing them as the responsible individuals they are, when we shift to noticing the moments when they choose to be considerate, kind, generous, we start to see them as the true positive beings they are and not react to what they sometimes offer us in their offness.

When we appreciate how far we, as a family, have come, from what we provide each other, and appreciate all the people that fill our lives, we can sit back in a warm glow of knowing that all is indeed well and wellbeing is ever flowing.

It's alright if we don't see eye to eye with our children and even if they don't agree with us.

We would never expect everyone to agree with us all the time, so why should it be any different with our children?

When we make the leap to accepting that our children aren't here to make us happy, or visa versa, we can rise to a place where we are together to support, to laugh, to Be, to care and to love each other, in spite of differences that may arise.

People change, grow, experience and experiment, we do as parents and they do as children.

Therefore, it's alright to express our differences, as it offers different perspectives and in turn it's alright to shift our perspective to the best feeling options when others, even our children, express their disagreement.

We can all learn from each other and when we grow together it is a wonderful thing.

Contrast is an incredible thing, it's just that often we forget how good it feels when we're in the middle of a stressful, overwhelming patch.

The relief, after a time of experiencing what we don't want and then finding ourselves suddenly in what we do want launches us into a state of pure appreciation and feels so incredible, far better than if we'd been in the spot all along.

Therefore, it's important to remind ourselves, when life seems a little complicated, when we feel OFF and frustrated by the tangled webs we can often find ourselves in, take it slow and steady. Trust that by being in that place it is launching everything to a new shift, a new perspective and because of that experience, Life will be all the sweeter.

We are part of a greater flow of life if we just
remind ourselves of it once and a while.

It is so easy to get caught up in the little things,
the need to control, to keep control, the need to
get things done and to juggle all the balls we
create for ourselves.

When we remind ourselves of the Universal
powers we can tap into, the Source of where we all
come from and allow life to be easy, we find that
things flow towards a happier state.

We can feel ourselves get lighter as we glide along
and problems we were once trying to keep our
thumb on seem to dissolve and resolve
themselves.

Breathe, relax and allow things to go well.

There will always be times when things aren't going quite how we wish they would.

The understanding that life is forever flowing allows us to give ourselves the space to acknowledge what's not aligned and allow things to shift towards solutions.

There will be periods when we are disconnected, caught up in the distractions of life, but those bring us clearer awareness to the connection we want to have.

By taking little steps, changing perspectives, allowing solutions to flow in, and finding moments to stop, appreciate, and truly live the life of the day, we stop the story of how things "don't go well," and leave room for things to grow, move and transform into the life we always dreamed of.

There is a hidden shift that lies within us, a subtle choice that is ours to make whenever we choose. The shift from wishing we had the time to do something, or wishing we were doing better at something...

to simply doing that thing, or being better at it.

The pursuit, or acknowledgment of needing the time or improvement is an important part of the process, don't get me wrong, but often we get lost in the wanting and spend too long in the asking of it.

Rather, when we simply look away from the computer and listen to our children, when we turn our focus onto finding connection rather than trying to find time for it on our to-do list, it is like turning a key to a door; suddenly the door flings open, relief settles in and we find it wasn't a huge ordeal in achieving what we wanted, rather it was there all the time and we were simply too focused on the lack of it to see it.

It doesn't always have to be the way we want it to be.

So often we can get caught up in the idea of how we want it to be, how we think it all should be, that we lose sight of what it is all becoming.

We don't have all the answers, and it is impossible for us to even imagine all the wonderful things that can happen to us and to our families.

Things spring out from nowhere, and it is only when we are open to them as a possibility that we can see them as an opportunity.

So too, when we allow our children to bring things in to the picture, and not insist that we know how everything should go, do we create a building ground, where everyone's instincts, ideas and inspirations are allowed to flow.

Our children are constantly observing, discerning, perceiving and then forming opinions and beliefs surrounding what they experience.

Sometimes it's a case of information overload, sometimes they perceive and interpret something that feels awful for them and sometimes they go through a period when life grows a bit stale and they are only witnessing what they've seen before and they need a new outlook.

We too go on the same progression.

When we see life as this journey we can reassure them, and ourselves, that life is always flowing and offering us new opportunities.

When it is overwhelming, there will be a time to adjust, when it grows slightly stale, new life and knowledge is right around the corner.

When we remember this when dealing with our small darlings, we can understand their flip outs, tantrums and upsets so much better, we can share their joys and sorrows so much more and ride the wave with them on the flow of life.

Along our own journeys we make new discoveries, connect to our Source in a passionate way, or find new beliefs or concepts that excite us and in turn we want to share them with our children, convinced that these will make their lives better, easier and full of joy.

Yet, our children are on their own journeys and come from a different perspective than us.

Whereas our childhoods helped form us, and our lives before parenthood were full of observing and perceiving, so too must their childhood experiences form their opinions and insights, from a different launching place than ours.

Therefore, rather than bombarding our children with what we want them to know all at once, we would do better to breathe, relax and live our own truths. The right time and opportunity will always present itself when our children wish to hear of our perspectives and beliefs.

If we are being aware ourselves, and conscious of our own connection, then we will be ready to speak when it is the right time...

for both us and our children.

It's the simple moments that, although often we take for granted, can mean so much to our children, ourselves and the fabric of our lives.

The simple conversations in the car rather than silence, the watching our children's favorite shows with them rather than using it as a time to get things done, the simple holding hands, sharing of laughter or even sitting quietly together, each doing our own thing, but sharing a familiar space in time.

Life with our children doesn't have to be intense and full on attention, rather it's about sharing a life, creating feelings of involvement and family; creating something we can all feel secure, safe and happy in.

Simple moments, which are often passed by, build up a life of love, laughter and security.

We can either wait for life to make us happy or make happy moments to create a happy life.

We all have the choice.

It's easy to fall into the habit of looking at life and finding the things that don't work, that get us stressed, just as children can moan and complain that they are bored or don't spend enough time playing with us.

As quick as a flip of a coin we can find ways to make life fun, including them in our activities rather than putting off play until we get life's chores done and out of the way.

We are what we think about all day long, and as easy as it is to beat the drum of discontentment, by shifting focus and playing, singing, skipping, dancing and sharing the moment with those we love, we see that life is a wondrous thing.

Even doing dishes can be something of a joyful moment when we take it as a time to play within our thoughts.

Take a deep breath and fall into this moment. Close your eyes and appreciate a moment in your day, it doesn't have to be a grand moment, just a simple one that will lift your heart for the moment you relive it.

It can be a hug, a glance, an exchange, it can be that first breath of fresh crisp air in the morning, or your cup of tea that you sipped this afternoon, it can even be this moment as you read this passage.

Simply, quietly, and for no other reason but to become conscious of yourself and everything you are, take a moment to appreciate and love the life you are living and who you are living it with.

It is easy to fall trap to the whirlwind life can transform into.

But by appreciating a moment every now and then throughout the day, we train our thoughts and hearts to truly live each moment and the more moments we appreciate the more things come our way to appreciate and the cycle begins.

It is a wonderful time when our children start to explore who they are and who they want to be, when they start to question what they believe, how they want to greet challenges of growing up and how they see their coming futures.

Although it can be tempting to guide and make suggestions regarding their paths, the only freeing feeling as a parent is to encourage and support them upon their ponderings.

Sure, some of their ideas may raise our eyebrows or may raise our fearful radar within ourselves and we could be tempted to speak against it.

But by being supportive, attentive and only offering our own experiences as insight we liberate them to be true to themselves and use us as a sounding board.

Act from love rather than fear of what the future holds for their inner guidance will guide them and they will see things clearer if they don't have our judgment ringing in their ears.

It's a natural thing for our children to have off times when their behavior challenges us and requires us to do a lot of deep breathing.

When this happens it's important to remember that having an off time is simply that; it's a moment of disconnection.

Disconnection is painful, especially when we haven't become numb to the state of feeling somewhere in between connection and disconnection.

Therefore, however tempting it is to demand connected behavior, it's time, rather, to introduce tools to find connection.

Our children's behavior is never a definition of who they are, so our moments of panic and fear aren't helping. Instead, simply playing calmly and focused, reading to them, talking to them and easing them from whatever torrent of focused thought they are on, can ease them back to themselves.

Challenges will always come up, for both us and our children and it can be easy to slip into focusing on the problem rather than allowing the challenge to be part of the process. When we shift to focusing on solutions, when we offer up what we see as the challenge and wait, deep breathing, to allow a solution to inspire us and while we wait turn our attention to finding connection moments of laughter and play with our children, we open doors which before had seemed closed to us.

Often worrying about our children is seen as good parenting. However, worry is simply trapping ourselves in a negative space, creating unhappy outcomes within our imagination and disempowering our children on their journey.

It subconsciously tells them they aren't up to the challenge.

Rather, shifting focus to positive solutions and looking for the laughter and glows in life, reconnects a family, giving everyone the room to grow and connect in their own time.

Our children will get disconnected from Who They Really Are. They will get frustrated, they will get annoyed, they will feel insecure, get mad and feel awful.

As parents it's not our job to make them connected all the time.

But by being aware of their disconnection, by watching for that sparkle in their eyes and zest for life, we can steer our day to day living to make connection easier.

When children are young they need to know connection often. They need to know that, feeling off is a passing thing, and be able to feel the difference so they can find ways to feel better.

When we get use to feeling off and disconnection becomes our default, that is when awareness is almost impossible and life becomes like walking in fog trying to find direction.

We always get what we push against so it's important to find spaces of relief when something bothers us.

If our children are focusing on something that doesn't resonate well with us, or spending too much time on the computer etc, we can fall into the trap of harping on it, worrying about it and nagging at them to get outside or shift gears.

When we find our own centre and feel better we can then simply offer them alternate routes, fun outings or distractions and allow for the right moment for them to jump aboard.

Everything goes through stages for everyone.

What brings us joy at one time will soon become old news and we will look for new journeys.

We are forever growing and expanding and we help our children far more by supporting the ever changing journey, than pushing against them doing what they feel inclined to do.

Our children ask so little really.

Listen to my discoveries and ideas.

Look through my eyes to understand my world,
Feel my love, joy, frustration, pain.

Hold my hand, my heart and me close.

Be careful with me and understand me.

I may feel off sometimes, when the world is too
loud or too much, but you feel off too.

Offer me love and time, consideration and
laughter.

For I came to this world to be with you, to learn
with you, grow with you and co-create with you.

We chose each other, let's not let day to day
stresses make us forget that.

Often it is our unfocused brain chatter that can convince us that things aren't going well.

Our run away thoughts can get us reeling and whirling and leave us feeling like the world is falling to pieces.

Training our thoughts, focusing our minds, holding a good feeling for longer than 17 seconds, so that it builds and builds more of the same and offering ourselves a safe haven in our minds, which we can rely on when moments get hairy.

When we remind ourselves that things usually work out, that doors usually open, that the universe is 110% behind us, that there are a million things to appreciate, and then we stop the chatter and laugh and play with our children, our spouses and friends, we reset our brain chatter, distracting it from its rant and start to tell a different story.

Choose your story, and you choose your day.

Allow yourself the balance.

It feels good to provide for our children, to create the safest place, happiest space and as many moment to moment joys as possible, but it will never feel good to sacrifice ourselves to offer it.

In fact, we can only offer the best of ourselves when we take time to connect to ourselves.

But in the day to day chaos of rushing around, keeping schedules, kissing scraped knees and offering hugs for hurt feelings, so often we can forget ourselves in the passing.

Allow the balance.

We can get in such a habit of rushing from person to person, that we can forget we are each a person too. We are all here for our own journeys, and we share this journey with the people we love.

Therefore, allow your journey to unfold, so as to be an example for your children to be someone to claim their personal feeling space, their deliberately created day and their lifelong journey.

There will always be days when we feel we just aren't good parents, there will always be times when our own stories, which are going around in our heads, seem to over shadow the connection we crave with our children, preventing us from truly being able to see life from their perspective.

There will be a lot of times when we go to bed wishing we had done better.

But our children didn't choose us because we had it all figured out before they got here.

We are co-creators with our children and together we grow, expand, learn and gain new insights.

Life isn't about getting it right or getting it done.

Rather, Life is the exciting prospect that we are forever growing and changing.

So rather than going to bed with an air of regret when days haven't gone as we wished, we should be quietly thanking our children and the day, for together we have suddenly desired to do better and in that desire we have grown and committed more fully to the choice of feeling good.

In the mad rush of life we can get distracted by life and simply move through the motions, struggling to find that golden thread to grasp.

When we feel this way simply asking ourselves each morning "what is my overarching intention", can refocus our day and our mental state.

An overarching intention is a fascinating term, as it offers the concept of a higher purpose, rather than an underlying tone.

What is the intention of the day, of the hour, the moment? It can be as simple as intending to appreciate the small things or to act from Love or to reach for joy, it can be as focused as to intend pure connection, to meditate, to pray, or simply to find a moment to Be.

A positive stated intention each day is a powerful statement to ourselves, the universe and the Source of all we are, and it's magic to watch it unfold throughout the course of the day.

Therefore, today make an "overarching intention" and see how much better you feel.

Perhaps feeling the need to fill our children's every moment is a relatively new thing.

For, with the arrival of smart phones and constant business in our own lives, we get use to being busy and often convince our children that they should be too.

So, we offer them games, we get them active, or in desperation we show them a screen.

However, our children are fully capable of finding the positive spin on "boredom".

Learning how to Be, how to stare out a window, trace shadows with fingertips and play in invisible worlds are sometimes even more important lessons than ABCs and counting to 100.

Trusting our children to find those moments, when their individual voice rings out for them, beyond others opinions or their own self judgments, is a gift we can offer them.

It is also a gift we can offer ourselves, for in relaxing in their scheduling of events to allow time to "be bored" we can remind ourselves to find that time ourselves and experience ourselves in a deeper, more delightful way.

Never forget to steal a moment of beauty, simply for yourself.

A passage of poetry, a pondering look at the new spring flowers starting to pop out of the earth, a sunset, art, music, nature, give yourself the moment of freedom to enjoy something of beauty for no other reason but to feed your spirit.

As parents we are well aware of how our actions are examples for our children, yet often we can get caught up in how important our actions are, how we need to justify all we do.

When we feed our spirits, simply for a moment, we allow the space to remember that this is our life too. We are living in each moment and there will never be a time when we look back and say we took part in too many of the beautiful things in life.

Our children will never suffer for our feeding our own spirits, only from starving them, for what sort of example is that?

There's no such thing as a bad child.

There are no brats, little monsters, or spoiled rotten kids.

Rather, there are only, disconnected, ungrounded, stressed, off, worried, unsure, insecure, scared, upset, sad, angry and overwhelmed people.

People.

At no matter what age, we all feel negative emotion, and at different ages we will express it in different ways.

By remembering this we can encourage ourselves to not label our children for their off behavior, in fact we can put energy behind not noticing it, or talking about it.

Rather, if we can offer opportunity for them to connect to their true selves again, to help them Be, to relax and laugh, then the off times quickly pass and we can recognize them for Who They Really Are, once more.

It's empowering to know that a slight shift in focus can alter everything.

It is in the busy times that our minds can chatter away, creating a negative focus on how our lives are unfolding. We can be picking up toys, ranting to ourselves how the house is always messy. While we run errands, we can go on a mental rollercoaster on how there's never enough time. Our minds can create a three ring circus, where we complain about everything without ever consciously sitting and thinking them through.

Life is never supposed to be a struggle, rather it is a flow that ebbs and moves, allowing us to experience all aspects of ourselves.

The slight shift in focus, that can get it moving again, is simply putting our attention to things that lift our hearts.

It's singing on the top of our lungs while we vacuum or do dishes, reliving every song from our childhoods, it's breaking out in a dance, or making funny faces with our children as we clean a mirror.

When we shift to focusing on fun and what is going well solutions appear and life flows on again.

Often life can convince us that, as parents, we need to hold the reins of control, standing on the outside of the action, denying ourselves the freedom in getting caught up in the fun of it all as a "just in case" mode of authority.

We stand aside, prepared to stop someone from getting hurt, managing relationships so everyone "plays nice" or simply remove ourselves as observers, watching the fun to appreciate it.

But life is about joy and when we allow ourselves to play, when we laugh together, joke together and relax into it all, we remind ourselves and our children that life can't be controlled. Rather we are there to help and protect, but we are also here to love and laugh, letting life roll merrily along. The next moment, the future, will manifest as it will, and by living a moment of joy, we create better ones to come.

Perhaps laughter and play is the best creator of all!

We all have our own journey, our own story...

all of us.

Our children have their own things going on, their own perspectives, priorities, mind chatter and as a parent it's a vital thing to be aware of that, avoiding trying to make our own stories their reality.

A family is a group of people, who are aware of each other's stories and try to make each individual journey a joyful one, together.

A family isn't an umbrella term, which overshadows a group, making their journey one, Rather it is a community, a support group, a play group, a fellowship designed in a non-physical, spiritual space to provide each other with a starting point for the journey, a bouncing off place for life, and a place to find constant love, laughter, support and care.

We are not here to fulfill the role of the universe for our children.

Rather, we are here to provide our children with the tools to take part in the magical powers of the universe to help them create their own happy lives.

We live in a materialistic time and so often we get caught up in trying to give our children whatever they need to be "happy". However, when we help them connect and find happiness in the moment, we help them bring everything they truly need and wish for, into their experience.

We don't have to take it on and feel bad when we can't bring it in quickly, for they are their own creators. If they are disconnected, then no matter how hard we try, nothing will be able to flow in to their experience. Therefore, we can only strive to connect ourselves to our truest selves and in doing so help them find their own connection. We are all co-creators, bouncing off of each other and helping along the journey.

We must try to never lose sight of the illusionary qualities of life.

The world is full of magic, of unseen forces, of a greater purpose and a higher joy.

Often, we can get caught up in the idea of this being all there is. Our inner voice can fall back into the habit of shutting out its true voice and simply reiterating the daily complaints and worries we tell it to.

When we take a step back and see ourselves, our children and our world as the illusion it really is, being pure, positive spirit, working on a vibrational level, that sings out with wellbeing and offers us indications of alignment through our own feelings, then we remember ourselves.

We see our children, not as young and unknowledgeable, but as spirits who aren't in the habit yet of telling themselves "No" or telling themselves of the impossible.

When we remind ourselves of Who We Really Are, we can see this time is but a stepping stone on the endless journey. Life is always what we make it.

Therefore, let's make it something spectacular.

When we find ourselves on a trend of worrying about the worst possible outcomes, we can break the rut by asking ourselves how often our worst fears are realized?

How often do we fret and worry, stressing through the night, only to find it was all over nothing?

However, the dial has been set and we usually find something else coming out of nowhere that knocks us flat on our back.

That's the simple way of the law of attraction, we set the dial with our focus, but it never sends what we expect. Therefore, with that in mind, doesn't it simply make sense to stop worrying and start to expect only the best possible outcomes? When we remind ourselves of the wellbeing that is ever flowing, that the universe wants things to work out and is constantly orchestrating various ways for it all to come out perfectly, we can give ourselves permission to let go, relax and allow it to fall as it may.

Life is meant to be joyful. It is only by allowing ourselves to make the perfect moment and leave the rest to Source, that things click into place.

Listening to our children can far exceed fulfilling their deepest needs; it can often fulfill our own.

There comes a point in an off day, that when we stop and listen, we can learn from our children and they, in their clarity, can help us adjust our sails.

When we can shift perspectives by adapting to our children's view, we create the greatest balance a family can offer, appreciating the tools they have and taking part in a true co-creation.

Oh the belly laugh... that burbling, sparkling portal to true connection.

Life is about joy and our children are so quick to jump into that flow of laughter as it rolls and dances, building upon itself and creating a ripple of uncontrollable, phenomenal, spiritually connected laughter.

Why do we resist the experience when we "grow up?" What is it that makes us feel like uncontrollable laughter, which stirs up from the pit of our stomachs and has us catching our breath, seem unnatural, like something that shouldn't be done.

We were born to laugh, just as we are here to dance, to sing, and to shout from the rooftops for the love of life.

Therefore, whether with your children in play or simply reading a funny comic in the paper... laugh, let it build, and with that laughter allow life to flow in and your contrast roll out!

Honesty with ourselves and our children is a powerful thing.

With ourselves, too often we can hide behind what we think we should feel or how things should be going. While, when we are honest with ourselves we can set ourselves free to expand and grow to the next step on our journey. Sometimes what holds us back from that honesty is fear of that next step, when really, a next step can be merely a shift in perspective, an opening of our minds and hearts to allow wellbeing to flow again.

Honesty with our children takes a different form. Often we hold back with our children, filtering information as a way to protect them or to protect ourselves from their reaction.

However, honesty under the comfort of love and well being creates a bond to a family.

When we all feel free to express how we feel and to be honest about a situation, we can then use that as a launching place for better feeling thoughts. When expressed with wellbeing, there is no need to linger in the truth of the problem, rather use the truth as a launch for the perfect solution, one that is pursued not solely by the individual, but in the loving arms of a family.

It only takes a day, a moment, to adjust our sails and return to the flow of it all.

Sometimes, we can fill life with "shoulds" or "if onlys". Sometimes it can feel like we do everything wrong and it feels like we are living a different story than we ever imagined we could.

But in truth, it only takes telling a different story to ourselves.

When we seize the moment and replace the negative chatter which can fill our brains with appreciation for what's in front of us in that moment, when we stop to give our children full on attention, enjoy the process and play, when we allow things to shift and move, acknowledging that everything here and now is here and now for a purpose, as a stepping stone and it will launch us to the next space sooner than we can imagine, then we stop...

breathe, relax, laugh and return to the connection we were so eager to get to in the process.

We need to trust in our children's journeys.

They came here at this time for a reason and as parents we can only offer them what is in our perspective reality.

In their own sifting through life they will find things, enjoy things and become passionate about things. They will be interested in topics that will raise our eyebrows and question.

We can offer them different perspectives, but they too can offer us the same.

It is truly a co-creation.

The old concept of the parent always knowing better is fading away and we can embrace the exciting path of learning together, experiencing together and enjoying each other's company.

Sometimes it takes letting go of our own plan, our own focused moment, and allowing our children to focus on their own moment for everything to fall into place.

If we don't want them to have tantrums every time they don't get their own way, then it's not really fair for us to have one every time they don't interrupt play in their inner worlds to get dressed faster, or eat their dinner quicker, to meet our needs.

Rather there is great joy to be had in stopping our daily chores and watching our children in their worlds.

There will be a moment in the play that we can interrupt or distract.

Sometimes it only takes postponing our plan for a few moments, even seconds, simply enough to allow our worlds to collide with theirs.

The door between will melt away, rather than us smashing it down and interrupting something magical.

Our children will always have off days,

just as we do.

However, we can support their journey by simply not allowing the off day to define them and giving them space to connect again.

When any person is off it is simply a matter of reminding ourselves about their true essence, that we offer the space for them to connect with all they really are.

When we define a person by what they are presenting to us in the moment, especially in a negative perspective, we hold them to that, restricting them from moving beyond and continuing along their way.

Rather than encouraging our children who to be "when they grow up" we need to start empowering our children to listen to their hearts, understanding that life is about the journey, not the destination.

If our children feel they have to talk about landmark events when talking about their dreams, then it follows that life will never live up to the expectation.

Whereas, when we encourage our children to enjoy being themselves in the moment, and dream of the feelings of life to come, it keeps the future fluid.

It's alright to play in the endless possibilities of life, visualizing and daydreaming, but not defining ourselves with them.

When we learn to trust our inner dialogues, our future unfolds with the unimaginable.

When we pass on that knowledge to our children, their future unfolds beyond their wildest dreams.

We should savor the sense of routine we've helped our children establish.

Be it night time rituals, meal times, or how we help them do the little things in life, by honoring them, we create, not only a sense of stability and security for them, but treasured moments we can hold in our hearts forever.

Often these routines can risk becoming chores, ones that interfere with our current activity or flow of the day, but when we approach them with care and love and let them flow from us, then the result is often a shift in the feeling space of the house.

Although "going with the flow" often inspires spontaneity and moments of inspired delight, for our darling children, going with the flow often means doing that which can be relied upon, without question.

Savor your small rituals, for they create happy memories and happy days.

There is a lovely release when we allow our children to grow and expand to new horizons at their own pace.

So often we get caught up in the "shoulds" of it all, the rush to change the things we dislike in our daily habits, the need to fulfill what we feel society is asking of us or the things we think our children need to achieve or learn in order to be ahead in life.

And yet, usually, when we release the need to force small changes and simply make a shift to see something in a new light, what we were looking for shifts with us.

It can be as simple as making a request to the universal powers and watching the solution unfold before us, or as easy as watching our children for the indicators of what they need as their next step.

Life is never as complicated as we make it and our children know that better than we do.

We all feel negative emotions sometimes.

They are indicators of the space between *who we are being now* and *Who we really are.*

Our children can often feel it's wrong to feel mad or upset and yet it's about what we do when we are in a negative space and the tools we use to feel better that can be past down to them.

Shifting focus to feel better, finding things we appreciate, getting rid of anger in creative ways such as going for a run or dancing to music all shift us to feeling better.

We do our children no favors when we ask them to suppress how they feel, rather we can bring their awareness to it and help them feel more themselves by encouraging them to choose what they think about.

To build a spiritual awareness within our children often means simply allowing them the space to understand the chaotic speed of the world that can race around our heads, and finding the quiet, calm peace we hold within ourselves.

Our children can find life so overwhelming, and often tantrums, moodiness or angry outbursts are simply a plea for quiet in their own minds and hearts.

When we can offer them a space to breathe, teach them simply meditation techniques, like finding a quiet spot, focused breathing, calming music and focused thought techniques we offer them a time to become spiritually aware within themselves.

Finding the contrast between the two worlds, the inner and the outer, and learning how to live in them both, is what spiritual awareness is all about. When we are aware of it, we can feel our way to our truest version.

By passing this on to our children, we empower them to find their own path, rather than teaching them what is our own.

We can trust that the universe will offer the right opportunities our children need.

Whether we think they have something to learn, something to offer or somewhere to grow to, we don't need to talk them through it, get mad or force them into their next stage.

Rather, as parents, we can only offer loving example, hugs, shared laughs and connection, then we can sit back and watch as they feel their way to better options.

Suddenly, a reaction will be a more connected one as they choose to move to a new understanding.

When they are allowed to grow and try out new reactions or lessons with freedom, they integrate them easier into the core of their beings.

So the same is with us, that patience with ourselves helps us grow into everything we are and who we want to be.

Love is a circle, and however wonderful the process of loving and appreciation is, and however uplifting and rejuvenating the process can be, the circle is completed when we remember that we too are loved.

When we allow ourselves to receive the love that surrounds us, not only from our family and close ones, but from the universe itself, we open up as the true beings of love we are.

Love is flowing to us all the time, no matter how often we may feel otherwise. Therefore, when we feel the sun on our skin we can feel the love penetrate through us, the wind at our back caresses sweet nothings to our very soul.

Life is full of moments to feel the love of which we are a part of, and by acknowledging the love coming our way, it moves through us and we feel more of the love we are sending out.

Circle complete.

It's simple to know and easy to forget:

our children aren't here to make us happy.

No one but ourselves is responsible for how we feel and even if they grew within us and from us, our children have their own journey to pursue. The flip-side to that is that no one is responsible for how they feel except themselves.

It feels wonderful to bring a smile to their faces or to hear them laugh. Play, laughter, joy and fun are definitely the ingredients to a happy family, but for all of us it is knowing the tools for inner joy, that only we can provide for ourselves.

It is finding the better feeling thought, choosing to feel good rather than stressed and overwhelmed, it is about sensing when we are feeling off and working our way to feeling better, it is appreciating and honoring the wellbeing and beauty in the world and rather than being caught up in the rollercoaster of life, it is watching its ups and downs, its ebbs and flows and knowing that it's all good.

This journey is an exhilarating thing and when we remove blame from others or from situations, then the ride can truly begin.

Sometimes our children seem to spin and spin, not quite acting like themselves.

We can berate them to connect, and in doing so disconnect ourselves, or in order to offer them the space to connect in we can distract them to play.

When we offer a game of some sort to our children, we aren't just helping them find their own inner connection again, we find our own.

We are consciously dropping everything else, no longer giving distracted responses to our family as we check email, do dishes or run errands, we are prioritizing our lives to be focused on love and play.

Stop and play and everything suddenly becomes right in the world.

Life is more than dishes and laundry, so much more than paying bills and the work at hand.

Under it all is a system of balance, of light and love that moves unseen through our lives and it is only when we acknowledge it's there, that it can work its magic in the world.

We are energy beings, made of positive energy vibrations. When we use our thoughts to spark more positive energy, we follow the flow of life that flows through all things. It can be as simple as shifting away from the daily grumble and focusing on our child's game.

It can be imagining and playing in our own thoughts, or getting on the floor with our children and tumbling and laughing together.

We are meant to dance, to laugh, to play, to sing and it feels so good when we take part in things, and feel good for no other reason but to feel good. However, it also feels good to raise our eyes to the moon and stars and know the sweet contentment of wellbeing flowing for all of us, in an unseen force we are all part of.

We are so multileveled, as people, and when we allow life to flow and take part in the joy of it all, we are everything we Really Are.

Our children's play is often their meditation.

When a child is involved in an imaginary world, it is with the understanding that other states of consciousness exist, the reality of that state becomes completely real to them, and sometimes when they come out of the game, day to day life feels completely different to them for a bit.

It's an interesting experiment for us to enter their imaginary worlds and play with them for a time. Sometimes, when we let loose our inhibitions, the world they've created does feel real and we too enter a different state of consciousness with them.

It's an exciting adventure to embark in a child's spiritual experience, and when we do, we step away from day to day reality which, when we take it, can ground us and refocus our perspective, tapping us into to everything...

We Really Are.

Doesn't it make stopping so much easier to simply remember that we are human Be-ings, not human Do-ings.

Although we fill our days with arm lengths of to do lists, we actually are made to Be first, and let action based living flow from us, after.

It's an interesting experiment, to suddenly stop, close our eyes and focus on our breath for one minute and then take a look at the world around us, appreciate the moment and THEN go through our activities for the day.

That simple connection, that moment in time, realigns us to everything that has to be done.

We can focus on each task with our whole attention, we can look at our children and hear them with our whole selves; we can be present in our day. When we don't take that moment to connect to our true selves and to our source we run around trying to get things done, and usually at only half power and unfocused.

We tell ourselves we can't find the time for those moments, but in truth we can't afford the time not to.

Nowadays, with our world so fast and our children exposed to so much, while, at the same time, shut off from so much due to screen time and flashing images, we need to be emotion stirrers.

To be Spiritually Aware is to use our emotions as indicators, but how can we offer that tool to our children if they are shut off from how they feel due to the world we live in.

Quiet times, playtimes, thoughtful times, laughing times, beautiful moving music, and funny images or goofy rhymes can all trigger emotion to play with and to help our children experiment in recognizing how they feel.

Using descriptive words, such as soft, fast, relaxed, busy, tight, can help describe the emotion so they can feel it within themselves and then learn the actual word for mad, sad, happy, joyous.

Offering our children tools to play with feelings and emotions are one of the greatest gifts we can offer, and in turn, it's not such a bad thing to review them for ourselves.

Just as when they were babes in arms, a child's sense of self is really a simple as feeling "On" or feeling "off". On is an indicator of feeling Who they Really Are, they feel like themselves, they focus, they notice, they laugh, they take part. Feeling Off can be as quick as a flash of lightning, simply over tiredness, hunger, an off conversation with a sibling who is feeling off, even simply a moment of boredom or an adult driven conversation which left them feeling left out, can throw them out of a connected "on" space.

But this simplicity doesn't end with childhood. We disguise it better, but it's still that simple.

We term it as PMS, we call it a rough day, we blame others, we stub our toe, and maybe notice the law of attraction building on our little off moment. But it is that simple. Off and On. On and Off. Connected or disconnected.

A thought can throw us off, but a thought can always bring us back On.

The best parenting moments come from when we
pass information on through example.
Therefore, when we make finding time to connect
to our truest version of ourselves a priority,
when we state that we need to take a moment to
feel more ourselves,
we are offering opportunity and awareness to our
children.
Often we can feel guilty to take some self
connection time or push it to the end of the to-do
list,
but by making sure we act from the highest part
of ourselves,
we claim being a Spiritually Aware Parent as our
pathway of choice
and act from a place of groundedness,
connection
and love.

Life is full of habits.

Our day to day rituals are created out of the
habitual state which we are use to; our thoughts,
which create our feeling spaces, which create our
home's essence, which create our family's sense of
self. Often, we can forget to stretch, expand and
try new horizons.

It's ok to feel something different than ever
before.
It's ok for us all to grow and create new habits.
Nothing is set in stone.
Nothing in our lives is stuck on a ball that just
won't stop rolling.
No decision, no life choice, has to be permanent,
unless we want it to be.

Today is a new day. Today can symbolically be
the start when yesterday's habits can be re-
chosen, or put aside for awhile, or forever.

We are forever defining who we want to be and
Who We Really Are, every moment of our lives.

Seize today, and tomorrow and each day, to be a
day of chosen habits, not ones you just got use to.

Sometimes means taking a step away from life to see where life is heading.

When we are caught up in day to day living, even our instincts can lead us to just doing what is expected, rather than inspired.

When we step aside, observe ourselves, observe our children and let everything go, we can feel our way to what we truly want our life to be like and shift to the vibration of it.

Life is full of endless possibilities and when we hold ourselves to the life that we've adapted to, we hold ourselves away from the life that is available to us.

Be easy with life, it is an ever flowing stream of new possibilities and adventures.

We aren't locked into any belief, structure or system. With just a refocus of thought we can relax, go about our day to day business and know we've released the dam that holds off our potential.

Our children have a great capacity for seeking out that which feels good.

They know it is the natural state and it is usually the motivation of everything they do.

As a child gets older, they start to plan the feeling for the future, they look for things or events that will make them feel good, rather than having the all knowing outlook that each moment can bring a new joy unto itself.

When we see our children planning on something that they think will bring them the feeling they desire, but within ourselves the plan feels off, it's not a question of locking heads in dispute.

Rather, simply saying "this feels off to me" and asking them if it really feels on/good to them now, if they can talk about the excitement of it in the now, if it's making them jive in the moment, then you know it comes from their Source.

If it brings them stress, it is then easy to remind them that wellbeing and joy flow through and all around them. Remind them to feel good now, and plan later; as we all can.

Our children's negative emotions need to be validated and acknowledged, but not indulged.

Children used to be told to smarten up, be brave, not to cry, and heaven forbid show signs of anger or aggravation towards their parents and elders. Negative Emotion that is buried deep by our children stews and lingers, growing deep within. When our children are upset it's vital to name it, call it what it is, and without our own negative emotion getting in the way, support them with understanding and compassion... and then help them tell another story.

When we start supporting our children's emotional journeys, rather than trying to keep them HAPPY for our own convenience, we help them be aware for their emotional indicators, helping them feel like themselves, or not, help them feel connected, or not... help them feel their way to the truest versions of the positive beings we all are. We all create our days by our focus. Bad things happen, and sometimes we feel sad, angry, mad or frustrated. By supporting our children's emotions, we validate where they are. By reminding them of things that feel better, we offer them a place to move forward to.

Often we can get frustrated with the idea that our children aren't listening to anything we say.

We pound and we pound at the drum of being unheard and create more of the cycle.

However, our children will often feel the same.

When we listen to our children, when we stop, look into their eyes, answer their questions, ask for their opinions and truly hear what they say, we stop the cycle of empty chatter.

They hear us listening to them and it creates a new cycle of them respecting what we say and listening to us.

A family who listens to each other,

hears each other.

A parent who wants to be heard,

but refuses to listen

will only create a cycle of frustration as they attempt control.

New thoughts, new habits or new choices can feel uncomfortable. Just as we stumble with each new step as a toddler, just as we tentatively touch and observe things with our senses when we are young, so too do we approach things that our new when we are "grown up".

The only difference is that sometimes we aren't as brave as we were then.

When we are children and we want a new experience, we jump into it with excitement, nervousness and enthusiasm. We understand that life is about living, expanding, growing and embracing everything in front of us.

But as we get older, we grow timid. We might fail, we tell ourselves, and we might look silly.

We might not like it. We might get hurt. We might not feel like ourselves.

Suddenly these excuses convince us to back down which goes against our natural state of being.

Life is about expansion. Life is ever changing. Life should fill us with excitement and enthusiasm and maybe a bit of nerves. Life is meant for living... just as we all did when we were new to it.

The art of spiritually aware living is to show up.

When we set the intention to live aware, then we open our hearts and minds up to the universal flow that is ever streaming towards us.

We stand, arms open, eyes closed, feeling the sun beating through us and wellbeing springs forth, while resistance melts away.

It is the simple intention of saying,

"Yes. Here and now, yes, I will listen to my heart and spirit, I will use my emotions as a guide to how connected I am."

"I will sing, while doing the dishes because it just feels better, I will play with my children rather than complain about their fun-noise."

"Yes, I will live, not control, or attempt to control, I will love, rather than judge."

To live spiritually aware, is simply to be aware, of how it feels, how to feel better and how to soak the most out of life, one moment at a time.

ABOUT THE AUTHOR

Christina Fletcher is the author of three books on
the topic of Spiritually Aware Parenting, has her own
blog and also contributes to a number of magazines and
websites worldwide.
For more information please visit
www.spirituallyawareparenting.com

23394075R00083

Made in the USA
Middletown, DE
24 August 2015